Knoydart – The Last Scottish Land Raid

KNOYDART
THE LAST SCOTTISH LAND RAID

ARCHIE MacDOUGALL

Lyndhurst Publications

Lyndhurst Publications Limited
1 Belasis Court
Belasis Hall Technology Park
Billingham, Cleveland. TS23 4AZ.

First published July 1993

ISBN 1 874766 01 0

Page make-up and output by
Alcazar Communications Ltd.
Newcastle upon Tyne.

Typeset in Palatino and printed by
PDS North East Ltd.
Seaham, County Durham.

CONTENTS

ILLUSTRATIONS

ACKNOWLEDGEMENTS

The publisher gratefully acknowledges permission to reprint copyright material as follows:

James Hunter: from *The Claim of Crofting: the Scottish Highlands and Islands 1930 to 1990,* (1991) (Mainstream Publishing Company). Reprinted by permission of the author.

Michael Lynch: from *Scotland: A New History,* (1982) (Century Publishing Ltd). Reprinted by permission of the author

James McDyer: from *Father McDyer of Glencolumbkille: An Autobiography* (1982), (Brandon Book Publishers). Reprinted by permission of the publishers.

The editors of the following newspapers are thanked for permission to quote from their original copy: *The Scotsman,* the *Glasgow Herald,* the *Oban Times,* the *Daily Mirror* and *The Times.* Norman Campbell of the *West Highland Free Press* is thanked for proof reading the text of the Gaelic cairn inscription.

Gratitude is also expressed for permission to reproduce photographs: Impact Photography (Inverness) for the photograph of the author, page xii; Tom Weir for page 4; Hulton Deutsch for page 8; the *Glasgow Herald* for pages 13, 16, 18, 19, 22 and 23; and the author for the cairn photograph on page 32. The map on page viii is reprinted by permission of the Ordnance Survey.

The publisher also wishes to thank Tom Weir and Ian Fraser Grigor for comments on the text. Thanks are also expressed to Norman Newton, assistant reference librarian, Inverness Reference Library, for checking historical facts and the spelling of Scottish names. Hamish Henderson is thanked for permission to reprint his song The Ballad of the Men of Knoydart.

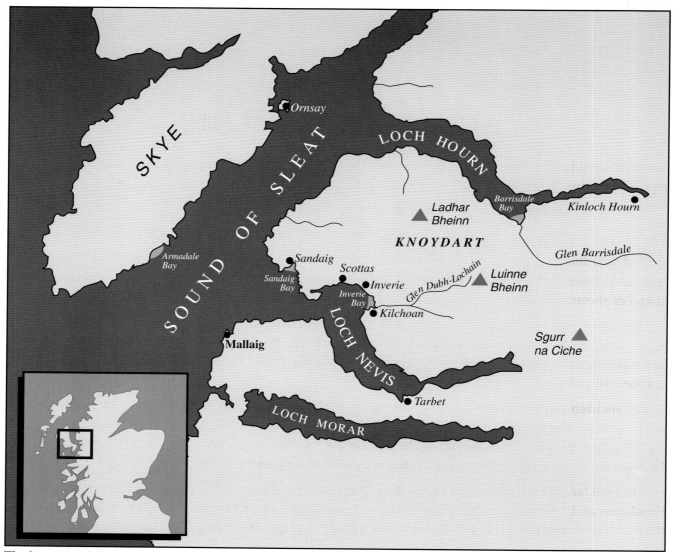

The location of Knoydart.

PREFACE

Knoydart – the last Scottish land raid. This is the story of an incident that took place in the remote and beautiful peninsula of Knoydart in Inverness-shire in the autumn of 1948. It is the story of men, frustrated by the changes forced on the place were they lived, who decided to take the law into their own hands and fight what they saw was wrong. They sought to claim what they passionately believed to be their right to form crofts and work land which was being deliberately let to go to waste. They asserted that their plight was the result of deliberate policies of their landlord and believed that they were the subject of twentieth century land clearance: this time to make way for deer and sportsmen instead of sheep.

The story is told by Archie MacDougall, the sole survivor of the seven men of Knoydart who made the land raid, and serves to remind us of their struggle to retain the right to live and work in the place of their birth. A struggle made more poignant by the fact that it took place in the aftermath of a war that had been fought to ensure that this very freedom could still exist.

The incident aroused much public interest at the time and was widely reported by the press. Although the land raid had little immediate impact on the way of life of Highland communities it focused on the issue of land use and neglect. Knoydart became synonymous with the age old problems of landlordism and indicated the determination of groups of crofters to redress old wrongs.

The 1948 land raid has not been forgotten and Knoydart has periodically been the subject of media speculation and discussion. With the recent change of ownership of the estate, Knoydart has once again attracted banner headlines in the Scottish press.

Rob Gibson, Scottish National Party Councillor with Ross & Cromarty District Council, has written the prologue and epilogue for Archie's story. The prologue sets the land raid in the historical context of Highland land use and neglect; the epilogue shows that in spite of events such as the 1948 land raid many of the old problems of land ownership and tenure remain. The long-term economic and social well-being of Highland rural and crofting communities can only be assured by the right political policies and commitment.

Following the epilogue come the lyrics of Hamish Henderson's stirring song – The Ballad of the Men of Knoydart. The book concludes with an appendix comprising extracts from contemporary newspaper reports covering the land raid, court actions and the public enquiry.

ABOUT THE AUTHOR

Archie MacDougall was born at Monzie, near Blair Atholl, Perthshire, in 1927. He spent the first four years of his childhood there and then on the death of his mother went to live with his aunt in Knoydart in Inverness-shire.

Growing up at Knoydart, Archie became acquainted with the activities of the Laird's house and estate. The extensive gardens and plant houses at Knoydart fostered Archie's keen interest in horticulture, which was to become his lifetime occupation. When he left school he went to work full-time as a gardener at Inverie House and remained there until 1952. After leaving Knoydart he became a fully qualified professional gardener and worked on many large Scottish country estates.

Working in the Scottish countryside gave Archie an insight into and understanding of some of the long-term problems of Highland land tenure and land use and neglect. Conditions at Knoydart under Lord Brocket's ownership particularly influenced his opinion of unsympathetic landlordism.

Archie is now retired and lives with his wife in Inverness. He still derives much pleasure from his garden and glasshouse and continues to follow the developments and events that involve Highland estates such as Knoydart.

Archie MacDougall

PROLOGUE

As one of the generation who was a child when the Knoydart land raid took place in 1948 I, like many others, came to the story through reminiscences of friends and the words of Hamish Henderson's ballad *'The Men of Knoydart.'* I started to climb the Highland hills whilst still at school and explored the history which has left so many empty ruins in the glens. It was when I became acquainted with the deeds of the Highland Land League while visiting Skye as a student, that the lie of the land and the waste of so many acres sank home.

The problem of the land in places like Knoydart is best summed up by a recent text about the Highland condition in the nineteenth century and the success of the Land League and its five MPs elected in 1885. They put critical pressure on Gladstone's third and shortest lived administration to pass the momentous Crofting Act of 1886. Michael Lynch in his *Scotland: A New History*[1] published in 1992 says:

> the crofting legislation did not produce a dependent economy; it confirmed one which already existed

It took another 30 years and the deep debilitating loss of the first world war before land hunger was finally satisfied after land raids by returning soldiers to their 'land fit for heroes'. A faraway government in London passed land settlement laws and transferred former sheep farms to crofters to meet much of the demand, but the slump of the twenties and thirties saw little innovation and much emigration to seek pastures new in Canada, Australia and the United States of America.

By the time that Britain was fighting Hitler agricultural policy was directed under the totalitarian powers of the wartime regime. The government demanded all out effort and Highland estates were commandeered for increased production. Again the Highlands were pillaged for soldiers and again there was little in the way of innovation or coherent voices raised in depleted communities to demand a new start after the war.

Inside the government the wartime Scottish Secretary of State, Tom Johnston, set up many committees to address Highland development. One of them concerned itself with land settlement and recommended the purchase of entire crofting communities so as to attempt reorganisation on profitable lines. Despite all this activity it is reported that over 500 people approached the Department of Agriculture in the five years after the war and were told that there were no crofts available.

In such an atmosphere, with the sheep farming sector being seen by government to be the mainstay of the Highland economy, little heed was paid to crofting as a viable alternative tenure. The government's main concerns were with the wide, productive lowland farms it was entrusted to develop. So when the seven men of Knoydart petitioned the Secretary of State for Scotland in vain, they took to the old ways of the land raid but in a changed climate compared to 1920.

The public campaign which they waged was fuelled by the resentment against the Knoydart laird, Lord Brocket, who had been an open sympathiser with the Nazis. Talk of nationalisation was again in the air as maximisation of food production was the government's firm target, but James Hunter summed up the political position in his book *The Claim of Crofting: the Scottish Highlands and Islands 1930 to 1990*[2]:

> …the Labour controlled Scottish Office seemed every bit as determined as the estate's pro-Nazi proprietor not to give way to the demands of the land raiders whose campaign, as a result, ended in total failure.

At the time it was reported that Arthur Woodburn MP, the Secretary of State for Scotland, sailed round the bay at Inverie on his annual voyage with the Fishery Protection Squadron and that was the closest he came to any concern for the case.

Rob Gibson
March 1993

IN THE BEGINNING

Knoydart, one of the last wildernesses left in Scotland, lies on the western seaboard of Inverness-shire. The estate of 60,000 acres is situated between two large sea lochs – Loch Nevis (in Gaelic, Loch of Heaven) and Loch Hourn (in Gaelic, Loch of Hell). The two lochs bite deeply into the mainland, forming fiords of spectacular scenic beauty.

This beautiful wilderness has had a turbulent history. In the aftermath of the 1745 Rebellion, with the clan system crushed by The Duke of Cumberland's victory over the Highland army at Culloden, the Redcoat army of occupation was under orders to pursue the rebels into the rough bounds of Knoydart, houses were burnt, and entire families loyal to Prince Charles Edward Stuart were subjected to terrible atrocities.

My grandfather settled in a place called Sandaig. He was probably one of the first shepherds to arrive there following the Highland Clearances, when 500 people were evicted and forcibly shipped to Cape Breton Island and Nova Scotia. These unfortunate victims were replaced by a huge sheep stock considered to be of more financial value to the then owner, Marjory MacDonell, wife of the Chief of Glengarry.

My father was born at Sandaig but moved to Monzie in Glen Fender, near Blair Atholl, due to the poor conditions of housing and wages at Knoydart. The estate factor would not sanction any improvement to his home at Sandaig.

I was born in Monzie but came to live at Knoydart at the early age of four years, when my mother died and I spent my childhood and part adult life there until 1952, when, through necessity rather than choice, like many others I had to seek employment elsewhere.

Inverie House, photographed in August 1968.

THE KNOYDART I KNEW

My recollections of Knoydart are happy ones. Like most people there, we had little money or indeed, material wealth, but we managed. Torrie was the name of the place where I lived. It was situated high on the hillside, wooded on the three sides with commanding views of the valley below. The scenery is spectacular in all seasons, even in winter the high mountains have a rugged beauty of their own.

Torrie, or in Gaelic, Torr an Righ, means King's Knoll. It probably obtained its name from Norse origin, for I believe Knoydart is a Norwegian word meaning Land of Fiords. I did not require much imagination to envisage a Viking king scanning the countryside from such a vantage point. You can see Loch Nevis, Skye, Rhum and Eigg in the inner Minch. The outstanding landmark of the head of Glen Dubh-Lochain is the conical peak of Sgurr na Ciche.

My early recollections start with my school days. The estate owner was Mr Bolbey, and on my way to or from school I met him on horseback. The Bolbeys were good people and they owned the estate for many years, it having been handed down from father to son. I can also remember hearing stories about the previous owners, the Bairds. They were remembered with respect, and to this day the houses they built for their workers can be identified by the letters JB and the date they were built. The Bairds owned the estate for a long number of years.

The Bolbeys kept a large working staff, both in the Mansion House and all other departments such as foresters, gamekeepers, gardeners, farm manager, carpenters plus a large yacht crew, and all answerable to the estate factor. Apart from local labour, they brought extra household staff up from the south.

There were at one time ten gardeners plus a head gardener, as there were large areas of lawn and wooded policies, and a huge range of glass containing vines, peaches, figs and pot-plants, and a huge orchard. Everything was kept perfect. I can remember those days.

I can recall hearing people talk of how they looked forward to the gentry coming north for the season. It was a great event when the yacht, named Vanessa, sailed into the bay, a happy contented community. The season always ended with the Ghillies Ball, a glittering occasion to which all the estate workers were invited, and not only this but the Bolbeys and their guests, who came up every year to stay at the Mansion and various shooting and fishing lodges, sent gifts at Christmas for the estate employees' children.

Now I started working in the gardens of Inverie House even before I left school. I used to work a couple of hours, you could say I was so anxious to become a gardener. I received very good tuition from Mr. Milne, the head gardener. Tuition which has served me all my life in the various gardens in which I have worked.

When I started at Inverie gardens the wage was 15 shillings a week, paid monthly. It increased by five shillings yearly until I had served my time to journeyman. The work was interesting but hard. Holidays were unknown. You started at seven o'clock every morning, lunch was mid-day, and work finished at five o'clock. Saturdays were seven o'clock till mid-day. Overtime work was never done, but there were some weekends when you had to attend to greenhouse watering and ventilation, and the boiler had to be kept stoked. There was only the head gardener and an old pensioner when I started and we were expected to keep premises where there was usually a staff of seven. At one time there were ten qualified gardeners and some women. There was a large staff of gamekeepers, forestry workers and farm workers, not including shepherds, and of all of these workers, the majority were local born labour.

Some of the household servants at the Mansion House were from the south, but a lot of local girls were also employed there. It was important to be guaranteed a secure source of employment for the future. However the upkeep of the estate became too much and Mr Bolbey was forced to put the estate on the market.

In the 1930s Knoydart passed into tenancy, and soon ownership, by a southern millionaire, brewer and landowner, one Arthur Ronald Nall-Cain, later to become Lord Brocket. On the death of his father he inherited the title Lord Brocket of Brocket Hall. In view of what was to happen it was ironic to think that Lord Brocket was the son of a philanthropist.

CHANGING TIMES

Lord Brocket was just 30 years of age in 1934. His credentials for ownership of a Highland estate were impressive, having attended Eton, played golf for Oxford University, spent some years as a barrister and a Conservative Member of Parliament. He owned land and properties in Hertfordshire, Hampshire and Maynooth near Dublin.

When he arrived first in Knoydart he was well received by the people and did seem to give the impression that he was going to carry on the estate along the same lines as the Bolbeys had done before, but this was not to be.

Lord Brocket's political interests were not only confined to the Conservative Party, he was closely connected with the Anglo-German Fellowship, a loose association of Tories and other well-wishers of Hitler. His connections with Hitler were known in Knoydart, and it was said that Herr von Ribbentrop actually visited Brocket while at Knoydart. I can remember that just before the war, the British Prime Minister Neville Chamberlain, was a guest at Inverie House for a week, fishing and shooting deer. Lord Brocket put on a great show. A great gathering, and a grand ball was held in the local hall.

Every estate worker, and all the shop keepers and bankers from Mallaig and surrounding districts were invited, and the police and the press were there. This was a typical Lord Brocket propaganda publicity exercise. Newspaper items of the time show a different side of his nature.

The Times, London, September 12, 1938 reported:

> The Parteitag is drawing to a close in an atmosphere of tension. Herr Hitler today was speaking to 120,000 of his storm troopers and SS men paraded before him. Sir Neville Henderson, the British

Lord Brocket with family at the official opening of Parliament, October 21, 1947. Left to right: Lord Brocket, the Hon. Elizabeth Nall-Cain, Lady Brocket, the Hon. Ronald Nall-Cain (and unidentified lady).

Ambassador, remained the entire evening. He attended the parade of the Youth Movement yesterday morning, and in the evening was guest of Herr Himmler, Reich leader of the SS camp on the outskirts of Nuremberg. At the meeting Herr Hitler had a friendly conversation over the tea-table with some of his English guests of honour. Those at the Fuhrer's table were Lord Stamp, Lord McGowan and Lord Brocket.

And in *The Glasgow Herald*, London, April 20, 1939:

All Germany is tonight celebrating Herr Hitler's birthday. One important feature of the birthday celebrations is the swearing in of ten year old boys and girls as members of the Hitler Youth. It is believed that with addition of this year's class, membership will reach 8,500,000. Major-General Fuller and Lord Brocket, Vice-President of the Anglo-German Fellowship, are the private guests of Herr Hitler.

Again in *The Times*, London, February 16, 1939:

Sir Neville Henderson spoke on Anglo-German relations at the annual dinner of the Deutsche-Englische Gesellschaft in Berlin tonight. Lord Brocket from the Anglo-German Fellowship in London also spoke.

Lord Brocket reckoned that many of the older local employees should be made redundant. One excuse being that it was getting too costly to keep up maintenance of the estate. But that was not true. The estate was really short of houses and most of the staff were in rented houses. Once the source of employment was cut off people would have to leave anyway, so the depopulation started, and the attitude of the Laird towards the local people hardened; even local children were not allowed to be seen near the seashore in view of the Mansion House. Lady Brocket personally issued instructions to gamekeepers that the orders were to be imposed. 'Private' signs and locked gates were the order of the day. Boat parties, campers, and hillwalkers were ordered off the estate. It was becoming a closed dictatorial regime probably in Lord Brocket's private thoughts; a jack-booted private wilderness materialising as his Nazi friends engulfed Europe.

It certainly suited Lord Brocket to keep Knoydart isolated, he did not allow the public access. Tourists and campers were turned away. One particular example of this stands out clearly in my mind, that was when the previous estate owner's wife, Mrs Bolbey, visited Knoydart. Her old gamekeeper was under instruction from Lord Brocket to keep every member of the public out. Mrs Bolbey was to be treated no differently from anyone else. It must have been a very difficult task to have to tell your previous employer's wife that she was not welcome. Sometime later, when Lord Brocket was in residence, he learnt that there were campers in the wood above the village, he immediately dispatched his gamekeeper to ask them to leave. This was to be as embarrassing for his gamekeeper as was having to tell his previous employer she was not welcome, for when he arrived at the camp he immediately recognised one of them as a member of Admiral Keyes' family, who were frequent guests of the Bolbeys at Knoydart. When Lord Brocket heard who they were he was furious, and accused them of spying on him, and ordered that they were to leave immediately.

THE RAVAGES OF WAR

The dark clouds of war spread across Europe and even reached as far as Knoydart. The estate became a military training ground by compulsory government acquisition order and Lord Brocket left for the south. All through the war he returned to shoot deer and keep an eye on the manager appointed by the Department of Agriculture to run the large stock of sheep which they had put onto the estate.

Ironically, in view of Lord Brocket's Nazi sympathies, there was a German air raid on Knoydart. It took place on a moonlit night in March 1942 not long after the Clydebank blitz. The bombs fell on the high hillhead of Loch Nevis and did no damage except to a few sheep and deer maybe. There were a few hundred troops stationed on the estate at the time and local speculation arose that they were the target for the raid. It is more likely, in view of the claims by Lord Haw Haw of German damage to the factory at Fort William, that the German airmen mistook their target aided maybe by some heath fires set by shepherds to clear heather. Several landmines went off in the days that followed the raid causing huge craters but no loss of life.

At the end of the war the military left Knoydart and Lord Brocket returned. The estate was to return to its old role of providing sport for rich visitors aided by the compensation which the government paid for the damage done by the military activities. Local gossip had it that fences damaged in the 1914-1918 war were claimed for again.

When the war finished the local men who were in the Services returned home, and were re-instated in their jobs as was an accepted fact all over the country.

I had by this time left school and was working in the estate gardens as an apprentice. Older members of the estate workers were sacked and the reason given was that owing to rising costs they could not afford to employ them. This, of course, was later disproved for in each case everyone was replaced by outsiders. I was one of the victims myself and before long was called for National Service.

The estate continued to deteriorate with less and less being done to maintain it. The decline had started during the war years owing to being short-staffed, but now all that Lord Brocket was worried about was to shoot as many stags as possible and ship the carcasses to the southern markets. It was mass slaughter; anything up to 30 stags a day were grassed. Lord Brocket seemed obsessed with killing, both the stags and the estate. Perhaps, when you look back on his circle of Nazi friends and their exploits, one could not expect much else.

I remember being told that Lord Brocket had once accused an old shepherd in Knoydart of not having thanked him for the venison he gave him the previous season, and by way of a joke added: 'If I was Himmler I would have you put against the wall and shot.'

Faced with the changes which were being carried out six local men, myself the seventh, became anxious for our future at Knoydart, if indeed there was any. We decided to approach Father MacPherson to draft a letter on our behalf which stated that, a century before there had been 1,500 people at Knoydart; now there were just 80 and 15 families were to leave before the end of the year. There were 12 usable houses lying empty. In June 1947 Father Colin MacPherson, the young parish priest who was the estate clergyman, submitted to the government authorities a development plan for Knoydart. The plan proposed a development which would increase estate population to 500 in five years and provide a welcome increase in domestic food production for hungry and rationed post-war Britain.

Lord Brocket blocked the plan. His intentions were clear. They were to further reduce the crofters' holdings and reduce the numbers of cattle and sheep on the estate. The obvious outcome of this was that many more of those employed on the estate would lose their jobs and their homes. Realising this, the mature population began to think of ways and means of staying in their homes and country. The only way was to take land for themselves where they could live in peace and security. So we decided to write to the Secretary of State for Scotland, who was at that time Arthur Woodburn, and with a Labour government in power we expected to get sympathetic consideration.

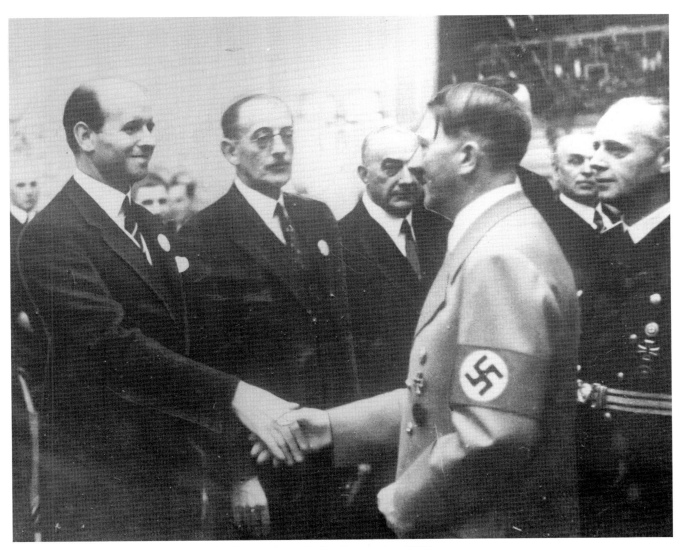

Adolf Hitler greets Lord Brocket at the Nuremberg Rally, September 1938.

The letter was acknowledged but nothing happened after that. Time went on and it became evident that letters were of no effect; action to bring it to public attention was needed.

In the summer of 1948 the men conceived the idea of resorting to the tactics pioneered in the days of the Highland Land League, and proposed to stage a land raid.

THE DIE IS CAST

On Tuesday, November 9th 1948, the following party of men – Sandy Macphee, Duncan McPhail, Henry MacAskill, Jack MacHardy, Archie MacDonald, William Quinn – marched through the village. They were led by Father MacPherson who was just old enough to remember hearing about the last land raids in his native Hebrides.

William Quinn and Henry MacAskill were both shepherds; Archie MacDonald was the estate carpenter, Jack MacHardy was a gardener as was his step-son Duncan McPhail. Sandy Macphee worked on the estate as well as on his small croft. All of them were determined to find a way to make a living for themselves in Knoydart.

I was still in the army, so I was not present on the day, but my claim was staked for me by my next-door neighbour, Henry MacAskill. On the 9th each man staked out 65 acres of arable land, and preparations were in hand also to raid the hill grazing land. Brocket was in residence at Inverie House throughout, and the next day petitioned the Court of Session for an interim interdict against the raiders. The petition claimed:

> On or about the 8th November 1948 the respondents entered upon cultivated parts of the said farms of Kilchoan and Scottas, to which they have no right or title or interest whatsoever, and staked out claims to small holdings thereon. Each claim was pegged out and contained a post bearing the name of the person who alleged that he was the owner of that particular small holding. As the action of the respondents in staking their claims was well organised, carried out in concert, and with the press having being duly informed beforehand, the petitioner believes that for some unknown reason some of the local people object to the petitioner's ownership of the estate of Knoydart and that further action may be taken.

Clearing ground above Inverie. Left to right: Archie MacDonald, Sandy Macphee, Duncan MacPhail, Jack MacHardy, William Quinn, Henry MacAskill.

I have the telegram I received from Father MacPherson which stated:

'Land staked in your name. Are you prepared to face imprisonment if need be, or relinquish your claim ?'

Needless to say, it was with my full co-operation and permission granted that Mr MacAskill, my next door neighbour, had staked the claim on my behalf, as I was stationed in Wales at the time.

After much publicity and public support, a fund for the seven men of Knoydart was started at Fort William.

The Glasgow Herald carried a report on November 15, 1948:

Land Claimants of Knoydart – Crofters Offer Support

A resolution pledging full support of the land claimants of Knoydart against whom interim interdict has been granted by the Court of Session, was passed by the Lochaber Crofter's Union at a meeting on Saturday in Fort William. The Union reaffirm their opinions that a bold and imaginative policy of land settlement is required for the Highlands and Islands. They urge that full advantage should be taken of the existing powers of the Secretary of State for Scotland and the Department of Agriculture to acquire land and form fully equipped small holdings. Copies of the resolution are being sent to the Prime Minister, the Secretary of State for Scotland and Members of Parliament.

A similar land raid, on a smaller scale, had started in Sutherland but it never caught the public interest that the Knoydart one enjoyed.

As it was to be expected, Lord Brocket did not take long in acting against the local population. He was really putting the pressure on. Firstly by issuing strict orders to his factor that no raiders were to be allowed to travel on the estate launch or have any supplies taken across for them. Also, no implements, such as farm machinery, could be given to Mr Macphee to cultivate his small croft, whereas before, when he was employed on the estate, he was allowed to get the use of any tools he required. Fortunately however, Mr Lennan of the Marine Hotel, Mallaig, who owned and operated the mail service launch, saw to it that we got everything we required. Mr Lennan, being a Knoydart man himself, fully supported our cause.

Everyone expected some dramatic action to follow the granting of the edict, but things did not go as

A pause for discussion on high ground above the village. Left to right: Archie MacDonald, Duncan MacPhail, Jack MacHardy, Sandy Macphee.

18

Postwoman Nora Reilly delivers the interim interdict. Left to right: Jack MacHardy, Duncan MacPhail, William Quinn, Sandy Macphee, Archie MacDonald, Henry MacAskill.

expected. *The Glasgow Herald* of November 13, 1948 reported under the headline:

Six Knoydart Men Abandon Claims

Developments arising from the seizure of land on the Knoydart (Inverness-shire) estate of Lord Brocket took an unexpected turn yesterday when six of the men against whom interim edict was granted in the Court of Session quietly left the farmlands after the receipt of formal notices from Edinburgh. After the solemn assurances given earlier in the week that the men would submit to arrest for their continued occupancy of the land, yesterday's events were an anti-climax. When the notices were delivered by the village postwoman the men were scything pastureland in a field a short distance from Lord Brocket's house. They stopped work immediately and, with the Rev. Father Colin MacPherson the Roman Catholic priest who has supported their claims, they examined the terms of the notices, which provide for lodgement of answers to Lord Brocket's petition within 14 days. There was a brief consultation during which Father MacPherson advised the men on the course they should adopt. He was acting upon the instructions of the law agent who has been engaged by the men. All six men had prepared themselves for the worst. Immediate action by the authorities was anticipated and the men had their clothes in readiness to accompany the police but instead they collected their scythes and other working equipment and went home.

THE LEGAL BATTLE

Lord Brocket's interdict forced us into court to fight our claims. I had to attend the Land Court hearing held at the West Highland Hotel in Mallaig, but first I had a lot of explaining to do in my Commanding Officer's office. After I had explained the position to Major Sewell I was granted leave to attend the hearings.

I remember arriving late in Mallaig station. I thought I would have to look up friends as it was not possible for me to get across to Knoydart that night. But as luck would have it, some of the local boys had hired a launch for the night, having attended a social gathering at Mallaig Hall that evening, so it was that I got home that night.

We were in high spirits that morning (December 22nd), going to the Land Court hearing, for we were told that we had a strong case and therefore reasonable hopes of success. On arriving at Mallaig pier we were met by a crowd of press men and photographers, and BBC reporters who followed us to the hotel.

So the scene was set for land raiders versus landlord and legal battle began. According to our lawyer, we were presenting a strong case. The lawyer and Father MacPherson had most of the talking to do. The findings of the Department of Agriculture survey of the estate had found that there was sufficient room for improvement and they thought that Brocket should consider a land resettlement programme. As the day wore on though, it was becoming obvious that we were not going to win.

Brocket's claim to the Court of Session had been that Father MacPherson had induced and persuaded the land raiders to trespass upon the said lands and had, since his appointment at Knoydart, consistently worked against him. Others observed at the same time that very clearly anyone working

First sight of the interim interdict. Left to right: Archie MacDonald, William Quinn, Jack MacHardy, Sandy Macphee, Duncan MacPhail, Henry MacAskill.

In Sandy Macphee's cottage. Further consideration of the interim interdict. Left to right: Archie MacDonald, Duncan MacPhail, Father Colin MacPherson, William Quinn, Sandy Macphee (standing), Jack MacHardy.

against Brocket was working for the interests of Knoydart and its native people, and the interests of the Highlands as a whole. Brocket did not attend the public meeting (everyone else concerned did). Instead his lawyer represented him, with a message saying that Lord Brocket, owing to illness, could not attend. More likely he had a guilty conscience!

The Secretary of State for Scotland announced that he had visited Knoydart; as a matter of fact he never set foot upon the estate. He went up Loch Nevis on a government ship and only saw the estate through binoculars. An independent expert reported that winter against the raiders.

THE END OF A DREAM

We appealed to the Secretary of State, Arthur Woodburn, who rejected the appeal. Then silence, no more word of anything further. The depopulation of Knoydart continued. The land raid had drawn publicity to the question of Highland use and the problem of landlordism, but nothing was achieved.

Brocket was now not popular within his own circles and beaten in spirit if not formally. Within a short period of time he sold out and returned to his English estates. His going was not regretted in the Highlands. Once it was in the hands of lawyers and politicians the land raid was doomed to failure, as in the words of my colleague, Duncan MacPhail, and I quote:

'Well, I was in favour of sticking on the land, you know, sticking on the same as they did in the olden days. But this lawyer got us round to thinking that these modern days such things would not need to take place; do it in the legal way, you know and it would work out pretty good. But I'm afraid that was our downfall. We should have stuck on the land and done as the old boys in the olden days had done – stick on the ground till they put you in jail.

We all thought it was a very good idea that it was going to be legal; but afterwards when we saw the whole thing and you look back and realise, it didn't pay to be doing it the modern way. Anything was better than the way it was. It was getting less and less used, Knoydart; plenty of ground in Knoydart – and good ground, but all that Lord Brocket was interested in was deer, that's all he lived for – to come up and shoot the deer. That, I always said, and to get rid of the locals.'[3]

That too was, and still is, my opinion.

At the time of the land raid Lord Brocket had a few faithful friends on the estate who were not very

LAND SEIZURES AT KNOYDART

Lord Brocket Granted Interim Interdict

TRESPASS ACTION

Lord Strachan granted interim interdict in the Court of Session yesterday against Alexander Macphee, of Kilchoan, Inverie, Knoydart, Inverness-shire, and five others living at Knoydart, from entering or trespassing upon the farms of Kilchoan and Scottas, which form part of the lands and estate of Knoydart. The petition was heard in chambers.

The interdict was granted on a petition by Brocket Estates, Ltd., Bramshill, Southampton, who are the proprietors of

1

Five of the Seven Men of Knoydart watch Mrs. Riley, postwoman, sort out their copies of a court order made against them.

THE SEVEN MEN OF KNOYDART GIVE UP THE LAND THEY SEIZED

"DAILY MIRROR" REPORTER   INVERIE, INVERNESS-SHIRE, Friday.

THE Seven Men of Knoydart surrendered today. They pulled up the stakes that marked the claims they had seized on Lord Brocket's land, though yesterday they had declared, "We'll go to prison before we leave."

But a feud has started in this hamlet of white-washed houses. The seven are Roman Catholics, and their champion is the Roman Catholic priest of Knoydart, Father Colin McPherson.

2

KNOYDART SMALL HOLDINGS CLAIMS

Answers Lodged to Lord Brocket's Interdict Petition

3

Secretary of State for Scotland and suggested Knoydart as a suitable area for land settlement. He also drew the attention of the Secretary of State to the fact that notwithstanding the provision regarding bringing up the sheep stock to 6000 by 1943, there were in July 1946 only 3000 sheep on the estate. The Department of Agriculture replied on behalf of the Secretary of State, but made no arrangements for settling the respondents or any other applicants on small holdings on Knoydart.

In or about February 1947, the respondents asked Fr. MacPherson to renew the application for holdings. Following upon the renewed application three local officers of the Department of Agriculture made a general survey. In or about June 1947 the Highland

4

Knoydart Men to Seek Legal Advice

There was a further development in the Knoydart land case yesterday when interim interdict was granted by Lord Strachan in the Court of Session against a seventh resident in Knoydart, in the parish of Glenelg, Inverness-shire.

be delivered to the men to-day. Meanwhile they have transferred their activities from the five-acre stretch of pasture land behind the village to another area at Kilchoan, about a mile east of Inverie, where they are draining.

UNIONS APPROACHED

The men have sent telegrams from

1. *The Glasgow Herald*, November 11, 1948.
2. *Daily Mirror*, November 13, 1948.
3. *The Scotsman*, November 26, 1948.
4. *The Glasgow Herald*, November 12, 1948.

pleased with what we had done, and such a statement appeared in the *Daily Mirror* newspaper, suggesting that there was ill feeling between the Church of Scotland and the Roman Catholics.

The article was in the *Mirror* on November 13, 1948:

The Seven Men Of Knoydart Give Up The Land They Seized

The seven men of Knoydart surrendered today. They pulled up the stakes that marked the claims they had seized on Lord Brocket's land, though yesterday they had declared, 'We'll go to prison before we leave.' But a feud has started in this hamlet of white-washed houses. The seven are Roman Catholics, and their champion is the Roman Catholic priest of Knoydart, Father Colin MacPherson.

In a country where there has always been rivalry between Roman Catholic and Protestant, a good deal of attention has been paid to the balance of power on the 50,000 acre Knoydart estate…

Ewan McVaddish, Lord Brocket's head stalker and leader of the Knoydart Protestants, told me (the reporter): 'Men who were friendly to me for years turn their heads when they pass me now.'

Mr A. McLeod, factor of the estate, said: 'I'm afraid this religious high feeling is going to keep on. I feel it must have some reasonable foundation in fact that these men are all Catholics'

Father MacPherson, watching the seven men scything rushes on their claims, became angry when I told him what was being said.

'It's nonsense,' he said. 'This is a story I keep hearing. I am prepared to say in a court of law, or anywhere else, that religion has nothing to do with my actions in this matter.'

The idea of it was that with most of the men being Catholics, and having the local priest as our spokesman, the whole exercise was designed to benefit the Chapel. I am Church of Scotland, and I made it perfectly clear at the time that never was there any friction between religious denominations at Knoydart. They all lived together as one happy community which respected each other's religious beliefs. The local two-denominational school, which I attended, was where you would expect to find that type of argument. In my memory I never saw or heard such a discussion, and that is how it should be.

Looking back over the years I remember various priests and ministers being at Knoydart, and they

COMPROMISE HINT IN KNOYDART DISPUTE

Brocket Estates Advocate Offers Land on Sandaig Peninsula

MANAGER ATTACKS SHEEP-BUYING POLICY

THE KNOYDART ENQUIRY

MR JOHN A. CAMERON, A FORMER MEMBER of the Scottish Land Court, presided over a public meeting at Mallaig on Wednesday, at which he heard views on the position at Knoydart Estate. At the outset, Mr Cameron said that he was instructed by the Secretary of State, in view of the conflicting nature of proposals for the development of the resources of Knoydart which had been submitted by various people, to advise on the position and submit a Report. He would take into account the social and financial position and he was prepared to hear any representations.

Last week he had made an inspection of Knoydart. He had previously been in Knoydart in 1940 when, as a member of the Land Court, he had been asked to submit a report on how the deer forest there could help in the nation's food production. The object of the meeting was to help him to send

The repopulation of Knoydart would not only be desirable, it would increase the productivity of the area, and would be in the national interest. Knoydart wanted an

holdings similar to those outlined in the scheme, and with a lifelong knowledge of local conditions, thought that the Knoydart scheme could be worked.

MacLeod replied now farming.

It had been ceedings that on

NO FULL-TIME CROFTING AT KNOYDART ESTATE

Commissioner Regrets Nature of His Report

REGRET that he is unable to recommend the development of individual

If at the end of ten years stock-raising had not maintained the stocking target and had not given an annual output commensurate

1. *The Glasgow Herald*, December 23, 1948. 2. *Oban Times*, December 25, 1948.

3. *The Scotsman*, March 26, 1949.

were always the best of friends and it is worth mentioning that in all social community activities, whether it be for children's Christmas party funds or sale of work, everyone mucked in. To read in the press that there was religious friction was a deliberate attempt to cause social unrest, contributed by trouble-makers. Such an argument would not hold water and if the sources of the rumour meant to impress Lord Brocket they failed there as well.

Lord Brocket is long deceased, and the only trace left at Knoydart that he was ever there is a monument he had erected in memory of his father. This stone cairn with a cross on top stands on a high rock overlooking Glen Dubh-Lochain.

The glen is empty now. Only the ruins of the homes of Highland Clearance victims remain, together with land on which the 1948 raid took place.

Six of the men who tried to take on the might of the landlord and the law of Scotland are now dead, remembered only by a cairn close to the spot where the events of those far off days took place. Of the original seven only I remain alive.

Now, the estate has a new owner who has sold off parts of it and very few people are employed. Time moves on and yet nothing changes.

There was a Land Raid Commemoration Committee formed in February 1989. Councillor Robert Gibson and Councillor Michael Foxley were the leaders who worked patiently for two years until they got agreement to raise a cairn outside Inverie village hall. Mr Rhodes, the estate owner, was approached but he had refused to provide any land for the cairn where it should have gone.

I unveiled the cairn on the 14th of September 1991. There was a celebration with pipe tunes from Ian MacDonald from Glenuig and the song 'The Ballad of the Men of Knoydart ' was sung I remember. A lot of people came to the celebration who had been away from the place for 20 years or more.

Looking back those 40 years I do not regret having been part of the saga. We only stood up for our rights. Had we succeeded, Knoydart would certainly be a different place from what it is today. It failed and the result was the death of a long established native community by an English landlord in a mini Highland Clearance.

It is my hope that the memory of Knoydart will continue to burn and be a constant reminder to future generations of the things that greedy landlords with similar ambitions will do. The depopulation of the Highlands will continue until there is legislation to have a compulsory land register and to stop the purchase of undeveloped areas of land by speculators.

The words on the cairn make a fine epitaph for the men who tried so hard to find a way to stay in the place they loved.

CEARTAS!

Ann an 1948, faisg air a' charn seo, ghlac Seachdnar Chnoideart fearann gus croitean a dheanamh dhaibh fhein.

Fad ceud bliadhna 'sann air a' mhodh seo a fhuair an Gaidheal seilbh air criomag tir a shinnsre.

Tha a stri na brosnachadh do gach ginealach ur de dh'Albannaich a choir a sheasamh le ceartas.

'Sann le fearg a sheallas eachdraidh air na laghannan ainneartach a dh'fhuadaich cultar araidh as an aite bhoidheach seo cha mhor gu tur.

JUSTICE!

In 1948, near this cairn, the Seven Men of Knoydart staked claims to secure a place to live and work.

For over a century Highlanders had been forced to use land raids to gain a foothold where their forebears lived.

Their struggle should inspire each new generation of Scots to gain such rights by just laws.

History will judge harshly the oppressive laws that have led to the virtual extinction of a unique culture from this beautiful place.

Archie MacDougall with the Land Raid Cairn.

EPILOGUE

MORE WASTED YEARS 1950-1980

The 1955 Royal Commission on Crofting led to the ineffective 1961 Act which failed to bring about any redistribution and reorganise the townships. Increasingly tourism filled the gap in earnings in some areas and the urge by the bright and footloose to leave ran its course. Even the establishment by Labour in 1965 of the old Liberal idea of a Highlands and Islands Development Board failed to deal with the land problem. When the Tories returned in 1970 they sought to sell crofts at 15 times their annual rental to sitting tenants but the bill fell with the Tory government and it was left to Labour to pass the Act in 1976 to allow purchase to begin.

I had been involved as a student with a land dispute concerning the Laird of Strollamus near Broadford in Skye through the Federation of Student Nationalists' Skye Crofting Scheme and began to understand the possibilities of community control of this most basic asset. In 1973 I wrote:

> Much eloquent work and sound work to back up the cause of Community control has been produced by interested departments in universities. But the intellectual alternatives need sound commonsense determination on the ground.

This emphasised the increased demand for Scottish self-government that has encroached onto the land question: the hope of most Scots is that a Scottish parliament will end the age old land problem. Other means such as communal control could replace individual ownership which would reduce the dependency and decline of the crofting communities caused by unneccessary individualism. The land question was now a political football between the Labour government and the rising power of the

Scottish National Party who promised to tackle it comprehensively on Scotland regaining her independence.

There was a growing belief that the standard of living possible in the Highlands and Islands could well match and surpass that of city housing schemes. Evidence of the late sixties and early seventies tourist boom suggested the possibility of a year round viable economy. The community co-operatives of Ireland were discussed and Father McDyer, the leader of the co-operative in Glencolumbkille was invited to the Isles.

He wrote in his book, *Father McDyer of Glencolumbkille: An Autobiography*[4], published in 1982, that

> If I have learned nothing else from my life, I have learned from the start about the effects of oppression and neglect in the West of Ireland. In my own way I have worked to counter these effects so that my dream of a Glencolumbkille rescued from the decay for which history seemed to have destined it, has been largely fulfilled.

Some of that optimism and community spirit would go a long way to help revive Knoydart from the sad state into which it has declined.

1980 to the Present Day

Knoydart's owners since the days of Lord Brocket have carried on with the hunting and shooting tradition. Over the years the people have slowly gone and today there are no native families left and so, when those who attended the unveiling of the Land Raid Cairn in 1991 arrived at Inverie pier it was to a community of around 60 people. The new community serves the needs of the estate as well as those people from south of the border who want to drop out from urban life.

In 1991 Knoydart was placed onto a slack property market by Major Chamberlayne-Macdonald. In November 1992 the newspaper headlines shrieked 'Ministry of Defence Interest in Knoydart'. This, coming as it did in the wake of the Falklands war, stirred a hornet's nest of environmental outrage and the usual concerns about unbalanced Highland development.

Two responses in the letter pages explain the dilemma of the eighties. The renowned Scottish climber, Hamish MacInnes of Glencoe, wrote to *The Scotsman* on St Andrew's Day 1982:

> this is a true wilderness area of Britain: a last outpost cherished by walkers and nature lovers and those wishing to get away from the roads. Knoydart represents a unique freedom in this age of the machine...it boasts a handful of fine mountains: Ladhar Bheinn 3,343 ft – another peak is called Luinne Bheinn, which surely suggests a place for the incarceration of Whitehall bureaucrats determined to destroy our Scottish Heritage.

And David R Jarvie writing from Edinburgh on the same day said in disagreement with local MP Russell Johnstone's cautious welcome for the MOD approach:

> The future of the Highlands depends on indigenous light industries – well planned woodland and timber operations, fishing and fish-farming, cattle, deer and sheep-farming, crops on improved ground – and controlled tourism...what we do not need is an increase in the military presence that has blighted much of the West Highlands from Cape Wrath to Machrihanish and from Stornoway to Coul Point.

Knoydart was seen by many as a unique heritage 'to be preserved for the nation' but as estate factor Sandy MacDonald said at the time: 'The problem is that the kind of fortunes which created places like Knoydart no longer exist.' Highland Regional council debated buying the estate and backed off from the costs, the newly formed John Muir Trust, named after the Scots founder of the American national parks system, pulled out, as did the National Trust for Scotland. Predictably the Scottish Landowners Federation called for the army to think again about a bid.

The failure of the public authorities was on Willie McRae's mind when he wrote to *The Scotsman* on 29th December:

> The Highlands and Islands Development Board has the statutory powers to acquire it and over the years to spend cash on it to bring back population and life and prosperity. I believe that, if the HIDB spurns this opportunity, it will be turning its back on its remit. How about it Mr Cowan? Have you the vision (and the nerve) to take it on?

They did not.

Despite the interest of Michael Heseltine, the Defence Secretary, the estate was bought in 1983 by one of the many property tycoons from Thatcher's free market paradise in the home counties. The Knoydart Peninsula Company was set up by the new owner Mr Philip Rhodes, who then commenced to sell off pieces of the estate in the fashion followed by English property companies at the time. Fortunately the John Muir Trust was able to acquire the peak of Ladhar Bheinn, the most westerly Munro on the mainland of Scotland, most outstanding of the mountains praised by Hamish MacInnes. The remaining 14,500 acres were put on the market in September 1981, the very month when the Knoydart Land Raid Commemoration Committee unveiled the cairn at Inverie.

Mr Rhodes had refused to give any land on which to site the cairn and it was only the efforts of Michael Foxley, the local Regional Councillor, who convinced the managers of a trust set up by a previous owner to offer a site for the cairn close to the village hall.

On the cairn commemoration day much of the talk centred on the success of the new Scottish Crofters Union, founded in 1986, which heralded a renewed vigour amongst the crofting population from Shetland to Kintyre. Crofters and their supporters can now see themselves in European terms as representing a basic component of a populated countryside and as the true preservers of fragile habitats.

This was underlined by the world wide appeal of the Assynt Crofters Trust in the summer of 1992. They had the unique chance to buy a Highland estate which was virtually all crofting land. They had a fall-back position following the Kinlochewe judgement from the Court of Session in Edinburgh which allows crofters under the 1976 Act to decroft land, convey it to a third party and not have to pay any development value to the landlord. Celebrations across the country and beyond greeted the news of their successful bid in December 1992. This will act as a beacon for land reformers after so many years of disappointment. The Assynt Crofter's chairman Allan MacRae said: 'It seems we have won the land and this is certainly a moment to savour. But my immediate thoughts are to wish that some of our forebears were here to share it. This is a historic blow which we have struck for people on the land right throughout the Highlands and Islands.'

For the people of Knoydart, now scattered to the winds, the message of success in Assynt is a signal that the long decline is firmly being reversed. When we review the last 45 years since the land raid the seeming inevitability about the disappearance of the Gaelic culture nurtured by crofting communities has been halted. But even as I write these words the news has broken that a Scottish registered company called Titaghur has just bought Knoydart. The press quotes them as saying they wish

> to reinvest in Scotland in areas of great environmental importance, returning Knoydart to its pre-eminence among great Scottish sporting estates.

So once more another absentee investor is using Knoydart for reasons far removed from the kind of hands on community controlled development which is needed for a Highland revival.

As the people of Scotland gain confidence in their rightful place as a partner in an expanding European Community, they will remember who it was caused the hard times of the past two centuries and who formed a land ownership system which has alienated the land from the people. That is why politically we are marching to a different drum!

Rob Gibson
March 1993

BALLAD OF THE MEN OF KNOYDART

By Seumas Mor

Tune: Johnston's Motor Car   As sung by Hamish Henderson

'Twas down by the farm of Scottas,
Lord Brocket walked one day,
And he saw a sight that worried him
Far more than he could say,
For the 'Seven Men of Knoydart'
Were doing what they'd planned –
They had staked their claims and were
digging their drains,
On Brocket's private land.

'You bloody Reds,' Lord Brocket yelled,
'Wot's this you're doing 'ere?
It doesn't pay as you'll find today,
To insult an English peer.
You're only Scottish half-wits,
But I'll make you understand.
You Highland swine these hills are mine!
This is all Lord Brocket's land.

I'll write to Arthur Woodburn, boys,
And they will let you know,
That the Sacred Rights of Property
Will never be laid low.
With stakes and tapes I'll make you traipse

From Knoydart to the Rand;
You can dig for gold till you're stiff and cold –
But not on this 'ere land.

Then up spoke the Men of Knoydart:
'Away and shut your trap,
For threats from a Saxon brewer's boy,
We just won't give a rap.
O we are all ex-servicemen,
We fought against the Hun.
We can tell our enemies by now,
And Brocket, you are one!'

When he heard those words that noble peer
Turned purple in the face.
He said,' These Scottish savages
are Britain's black disgrace.
It may be true that I let some few
Thousand acres go to pot,
But each one I'd give to a London spiv,
Before any Goddam Scot!'

'You're a crowd of Tartan Bolshies!
But I'll soon have you licked,
I'll write to the Court of Session,

For an Interim Interdict.
I'll write to my London lawyers,
And they will understand'
'Och to Hell with your London lawyers,
We want our Highland Land.'

When Brocket heard these fighting words,
He fell down in a swoon,
But they splashed his jowl with uisge,
And he woke up mighty soon,
And he moaned, 'These Dukes of Sutherland
Were right about the Scot.
If I had my way I'd start today,
And clear the whole damn lot!'

Then up spoke the men of Knoydart:
'You have no earthly right,
For this is the land of Scotland,
And not the Isle of Wight.
When Scotland's proud Fianna,
With ten thousand lads is manned,
We will show the world that Highlanders
Have a right to Scottish Land.'

'You may scream and yell, Lord Brocket –
You may rave and stamp and shout,
But the lamp we lit in Knoydart
Will never now go out.
For Scotland's on the march my boys –
We think it won't be long.
Roll on the day when the Knoydart Way
Is Scotland's battle song.'

NOTES

Bibliographic details of books quoted in the text.

1. *Scotland: A New History,* by Michael Lynch. Century Publishing Ltd., revised edition 1992, ISBN 0 7126 9893 0.

2. *The Claim of Crofting: the Scottish Highlands and Islands 1930 to 1990,* by James Hunter. Mainstream Publishing Company, 1991, ISBN 1 85158 329 7.

3. *Odyssey: Voices from Scotland's Recent Past,* volume 1, edited by Billy Kay. Polygon Books, 1980, ISBN 0 904919 47 1.

4. *Father McDyer of Glencolumbkille: An Autobiography,* by James McDyer. Brandon Book Publishers, 1982, ISBN 0 86322 001 0.

Other recommended titles.

1. *Making of the Crofting Community,* by James Hunter. John Donald Publishers Ltd., 1976, ISBN 0 85976 014 6.

2. *A History of the Highland Clearances: Agrarian Transformation and the Evictions 1746 – 1886,* by Eric Richards. Croom Helm, 1982, (now with Routledge, Chapman & Hall Ltd.) ISBN 0 7099 2249 3.

3. *Canadian History before Confederation: Essays and Interpretations,* edited by J. M. Bumsted, 2nd edition. Irwin-Dorsey, 1979. ISBN 0 256 02136 8.

4. *The People's Clearance: Highland Emigration to British North America. 1770 – 1815,* by J. M. Bumsted. Edinburgh University Press, 1982. ISBN 0 85224 419 3.

APPENDIX

The appendix comprises a selection of extracts from contemporary newspaper reports of the land raid, the granting of the interim interdict by the Court of Session in Edinburgh, the Knoydart men's response, the subsequent public enquiry at Mallaig and the report of that enquiry which finally closed the matter.

The newspaper articles clearly indicate the considerable amount of local and national sympathy and support for the Knoydart men's actions. The reports also indicate the somewhat unsympathetic response of both the local landlord and the chairman of the public enquiry, the latter's attitude resulting in the Knoydart men ultimately losing their case.

The events at Knoydart were first reported by both *The Glasgow Herald* and *The Scotsman* on November 11, 1948. The *Herald* published the following article:

Land Seizures at Knoydart

Lord Strachan granted interim interdict in the Court of Session yesterday against Alexander Macphee of Kilchoan, Inverie, Knoydart, Inverness-shire and five others living at Knoydart from entering or trespassing upon the farms of Kilchoan and Scottas which form part of the lands and estate of Knoydart. The petition was heard in Chambers.

The interdict was granted on a petition by Brocket Estates Ltd., Bramshill, Southampton, who are proprietors of certain lands in the county including the two farms. They state that, on or about Monday the respondents entered upon cultivated parts of the two farms to which they had no right, title or interest whatsoever and staked out claims to small holdings thereon…

The Scotsman of the same day carried a major report:

Land Seized at Knoydart

Interim Interdict Against Six Former Estate Employees

Father MacPherson, 31 year old priest, who went to Knoydart in 1942, told me (the reporter) that he had written to the Secretary of State for Scotland in 1946 broaching the question of developing the Knoydart estate. It had been surveyed by Department of Agriculture officials and later for the Highland Advisory Panel. Knoydart had been requisitioned during the war but a recommendation that it should be requisitioned again last year had not been carried out. A final request for the specific holdings now claimed had been sent about three weeks ago, he added, but no reply had been received. When I saw Lord Brocket in Mallaig shortly before his departure yesterday morning, he told me that the Knoydart estate, which he has owned since 1932, extends to 52,000 acres. He had been in touch with the Department of Agriculture and the Agricultural Executive Committee and he had a scheme – which had their approval – for developing farming and forestry. Neither of these, he pointed out, could be carried out without labour and houses.

He denied any suggestion that he was trying to get rid of the local population, and mentioned that his wage bill in Knoydart was £6,000 per year.

Events are being watched with keen interest in the surrounding area. While I have heard a good deal of sympathy expressed for the men, there are many who do not see how they can maintain themselves and their families even if they were allowed to retain possession of the lands which they have claimed.

On November 12, 1948 *The Glasgow Herald* carried another report:

Knoydart Men to seek Legal Advice

There was a further development in the Knoydart land case yesterday when interim interdict was granted by Lord Strachan against a seventh resident in Knoydart, in the parish of Glenelg Inverness-shire.

As in the case of the other six residents against whom interdict was granted on Wednesday the seventh respondent Henry MacAskill, Torrie, Knoydart – had staked out a claim to a portion of the lands of Knoydart and the petition which was presented by Brocket Estates Ltd., was against his entering or trespassing on Lord Brocket's 52,000 acre estate of Knoydart. He also was given 14 days within which to lodge answers.

The seven men have decided to engage a lawyer, it was stated yesterday by the Rev Father Colin MacPherson, parish priest at Inverie who has taken an active part in the support of the men. He said that he also intended to ask for the support of Sir Murdoch MacDonald, M.P. for Inverness and Mr Malcolm MacMillan, M.P. for the Western Isles…

The *Daily Mirror* reported on November 13, 1948:

The Seven Men Of Knoydart Give Up The Land They Seized

…Then Gaelic speaking Mrs Riley, the postwoman, trudged down the muddy lane. She carried copies of the order (interim interdict) – one for every man.

Father MacPherson explained the legal phrases to the men. And they pulled the stakes from the ground and walked home through the rain.

The lodging of their defence in the Court of Session was substantially covered by both *The Scotsman* and *The Glasgow Herald* on November 26, 1948.

The *Herald* published the following report:

Knoydart Men's Answers – Voicing 'Demand for Land'

Contending that the interim interdict granted against them by Lord Strachan in the Court of Session a fortnight ago should be recalled, six of the seven 'men of Knoydart' yesterday lodged answers in the court.

They claimed that they were within their rights in terms of the Small Landholders (Scotland) Act 1911 and the Land Settlement (Scotland) Act 1919 in visiting, without damaging growing crops or fences, Knoydart estate for the purpose of viewing it and indicating by means of posts areas which, in their opinion, were particularly suitable for small holdings. The six respondents, against whom action was taken by Brocket Estates, Ltd, Bramshill, Southampton, explain that they were thus demonstrating to, and impressing upon, the Department of Agriculture the existence of a demand for small holdings in the area and that there was suitable land available......

On the same day *The Scotsman* published its report:

Knoydart Small Holdings Claim

They (the respondents) aver that there is a demand for small holdings on the estate of Knoydart and that they and about 43 other persons, have forwarded applications and requisitions to the Department of Agriculture to form new holdings on the estate…

It continued

…The respondents believe and aver that since the acquisition of the estate by Lord Brocket down to the outbreak of war in 1939 the food production capabilities steadily decreased and that it was the policy of Lord Brocket to convert Knoydart from a sheep rearing area into a purely sporting estate and, as part of this policy, to reduce the number of people living on the estate. After the outbreak of war in 1939 Lord Brocket was, in the interests of food production, called upon by the Department of Agriculture for Scotland to increase the number of sheep on Knoydart estate, but his efforts in this respect were apparently so unsatisfactory to the Department that the estate was requisitioned under the Emergency Powers Acts. After representations to the Department the requisition was removed in or about 1941, but only on the condition that Lord Brocket brought by 1943 the number of ewes on the estate up to 6000. Notwithstanding this condition, respondents aver, Lord Brocket never succeeded in bringing the number of ewes to 6000, and in or about July 1946 the respondents asked the Rev. Colin MacPherson, who was Roman Catholic priest at Inverie, to assist them in obtaining small holdings upon the estate.

The Rev. Fr. MacPherson wrote to the Secretary of State for Scotland and suggested Knoydart as a suitable area for land settlement. He also drew the attention of the Secretary of State to the fact that, notwithstanding the provision regarding bringing up the sheep stock to 6000 by 1943, there were in July 1946 only 3000 sheep on the estate. The Department of Agriculture replied on behalf of the Secretary of State, but made no arrangements for settling the respondents or any other applicants on small holdings in Knoydart…

By this time the Knoydart affair had reached the House of Commons. Both *The Scotsman* and *The Glasgow Herald* reported on November 26, 1948 the question asked by Mr J L Williams (Lab. Kelvingrove) of Arthur Woodburn, Secretary of State for Scotland. The Secretary's response was also published.

The following report appeared in *The Scotsman:*

Knoydart Resources

...Mr Woodburn in a written reply said – 'In view of the conflicting nature of proposals for the development of the resources of the Knoydart peninsula which have been submitted by different interests in the locality, I have decided after consultation with the Highlands Advisory Panel to invite Mr John Cameron, formerly of the Land Court, to examine the position and to advise on the best means of securing the full development of the resources of the area, taking into account the social, economic and financial issues involved...'

The public enquiry into the Knoydart affair was held in Mallaig on December 22, 1948. The enquiry was chaired by John Archibald Cameron, former Commissioner of the Land Court. He had been appointed by Mr. Arthur Woodburn, Secretary of State for Scotland. Lord Brocket was represented by Mr. C.J.D. Shaw, advocate. The seven Knoydart men were represented by Mr John Shaw MacKinnon, solicitor, Edinburgh.

The enquiry was extensively reported in the Scottish press. *The Glasgow Herald* of December 23, 1948, carried a large article:

Compromise Hint in Knoydart Dispute
Brocket Estates' Advocate Offers Land at Sandaig
Manager Attacks Sheep Buying Policy

Mr C.J.D. Shaw, advocate, acting on behalf of the Brocket Estates, Ltd, hinted here today at a compromise in the Knoydart estate dispute. He told a meeting of interested parties that land was available for crofting on the Sandaig Peninsula, with an outrun for sheep behind.

A meeting was called by Mr. John A. Cameron, a Perthshire hill farmer and former member of the Scottish Land Court, who has been asked by the Secretary of State for Scotland to advise him on the best methods of securing the full development of the estate...

...Mr Ian MacLeod, manager of the Knoydart estate since 1947, answering a series of pointed questions by Mr Cameron, agreed that nothing was done by the estate from 1939 to 1947 to contribute to the country's food supply.

The long article went on and concluded as follows:

> Mr C.J.D. Shaw on behalf of Brocket Estates, Ltd, said: 'I do ask you,' he said to Mr Cameron, 'not to recommend the driving out of capital and enterprise from the work which it is doing there now but to recommend a compromise which is in the financial and economic interests of the area and from a social point of view will bring the two interests together'

> The enquiry was then concluded, and Mr Cameron will make his report to the Secretary of State in due course.

Towards the end of March, 1949, Mr Cameron announced recommendations for the Knoydart estate. Once again the topic received extensive press coverage and comment.

The *Oban Times* of April 2, 1949 carried the following report:

Small Holdings Scheme for Knoydart Rejected
Report recommends Development as Single Unit

Schemes for the breaking up of the Knoydart estate into small holdings have been rejected by Mr John A. Cameron who was appointed at the end of last year by the Secretary of State for Scotland to report on proposals for the development of the resources of the peninsula, taking into account the social, economic and financial issues involved…

In his report, which was published at the end of last week, Mr. Cameron expresses the view that if the estate was broken up into separate units on the lines broadly indicated in the Department of Agriculture for Scotland's scheme, featuring 19 holdings or under the Fr. MacPherson scheme featuring 40 holdings, the cost would be out of proportion to the production results and the livelihood of the crofters would be certainly insecure and with little comfort…

He recommends instead that the estate should be developed as a single unit under one direction preferably with a limited forestry development to be undertaken by Brocket Estates Ltd…

The report continued and gave much detail about the arguments for and against the breaking up of the estate. Significantly, it ended with the following paragraph:

'I regret the nature of my report as I am well aware that the natural instinct of the Highlanders is to have their own individual holdings, both for the cultivation and the raising of stock, rather than for wage earning employment, but I cannot see that it would be in their interests to recommend the development of such holdings in Knoydart.'

Perhaps not surprisingly Lord Brocket agreed with the report. *The Scotsman* of March 22, 1949 published a brief item on his comments:

Lord Brocket Agrees

Interviewed last night, Lord Brocket said he would not like to comment on the report until he had an opportunity to study it in detail. 'It has always been my contention,' he declared, 'that owing to the geographical situation it would be impossible to run the estate except as one unit. Mr Cameron has backed my contention in his report.'…

In the same report, however, the Rev. T. M. Murchison, Glasgow, chairman of the Highland Development League gave an opposite point of view:

…the report seemed unsatisfactory from the point of view of development in the Highlands.

The general acceptance of Mr Cameron's principle of regarding the matter from the viewpoint of economic development might prove dangerous. There was more to be considered. They had to think in terms of generations. The population of much of the Highlands had fallen by half in the past 40 years and in another 50 or 100 years there would scarcely be a family left in some places. That seemed to him to justify the view that more than merely economic questions should be considered. If communications were poor it was because of a long period of neglect in which much of the area had been allowed to become derelict. There was no hope of development in the Highlands unless the State was prepared to invest a good deal of money for such purposes.

The Knoydart affair then ceased to attract much newspaper attention; however for the people of Knoydart the problems of a declining agricultural community remained. The significance of what happened in that remote peninsula has echoes in recent events. The welfare of other Highland communities continues to be threatened by the decline, break up and sale of large estates.